LEOAPE'S™

GALAXY OF BLACK INVENTORS

The People Who Made the World a Better Place

LeoApe Motto:

"Always respect everyone. Never bully anyone."

LeoApe's™ Galaxy of Black Inventors: The People Who Made the World a Better Place celebrates the diversity of black inventors, and it shows how their inventions have benefited people all over the world. This book is a great way to teach children about the importance of diversity and inclusion, and that anything is possible if they work hard and never give up on their dreams.

Most of all, this book shows that black people have made significant contributions to society that affect our daily lives today!

Disclaimer

Images are for likeness only and do not represent copies of the initial inventions.

The year is 2023, and the world is a very different place than it was just a few decades ago. Thanks to the ingenuity and creativity of black inventors, our lives are now made easier and more convenient in countless ways

Take the traffic light, for example. Invented by Garrett Morgan in 1923, the traffic light has made our streets safer and more efficient. Morgan was also a pioneer in the field of gas masks, and his invention helped to save countless lives during World War I.

Another important invention by a black inventor is the pacemaker. Invented by Earl Bakken in 1957, the pacemaker has helped to extend the lives of mil– lions of people with heart disease. Bakken was also a co–founder of Medtronic, one of the world's leading medical device companies

These are just two examples of the many ways that black inventors have made our lives better. Their ingenuity and creativity have helped to improve our health, our safety, and our overall quality of life.

The Galaxy of Black Inventors is a presentation of perseverance and over– coming adversity. In a world where they were often underrepresented and discriminated against, black inventors found ways to succeed and make their mark on the world.

One such inventor was Lewis Latimer, who invented the carbon filament for the light bulb. Latimer was born into slavery in 1848, but he was able to escape to freedom and eventually become a successful inventor. His invention made light bulbs more affordable and efficient, and it helped to usher in the age of electric lighting.

Another inspiring story is that of Shirley Chisholm, who was the first black woman elected to Congress. Chisholm was a tireless advocate for civil rights and women's rights, and she was also a brilliant inventor. She patented a hair–care product that helped to improve the lives of black women all over the world.

The stories of these black inventors are a reminder that anything is possible if you set your mind to it. They faced discrimination and obstacles, but they never gave up on their dreams. Their inventions have made our lives better, and they continue to inspire us today.

AIR CONDITIONING UNIT: Frederick McKinley Jones invented the first portable air conditioning unit in 1949. This invention made it possible to cool homes and businesses in hot climates, and it has helped to improve the comfort and productivity of millions of people.

AUTOMATIC GEAR SHIFT: Richard Spikes invented the first automatic gear shift in 1932. This invention made it easier to drive cars, and it has helped to make driving safer and more efficient.

BABY BUGGY: Lewis Latimer invented the first baby buggy in 1889. This invention made it easier for parents to transport their children, and it has helped to improve the safety and well—being of children.

BICYCLE FRAME: John W. Goode invented the first bicycle frame made of steel in 1895. This invention made bicycles lighter and more durable, and it has helped to make bicycling more popular.

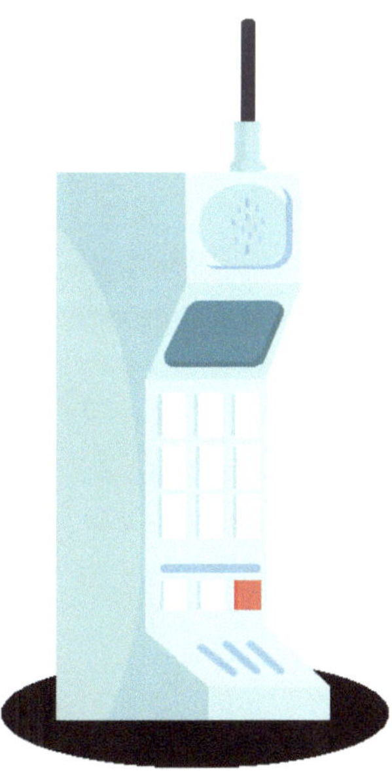

CELLULAR PHONE: Martin Cooper invented the first cellular phone in 1973. This invention has revolutionized the way we communicate, and it has helped to keep us connected with friends and family no matter where we are.

CLOTHES DRYER: George T. Washington invented the first clothes dryer in 1892. This invention made it easier to dry clothes, and it has helped to save people time and energy.

CURTAIN ROD: Granville T. Woods invented the first curtain rod in 1878. This invention made it easier to hang curtains, and it has helped to improve the appearance of homes and businesses.

CURTAIN ROD SUPPORT: Granville T. Woods invented the first curtain rod sup—port in 1878. This invention made it easier to hang curtains, and it has helped to improve the appearance of homes and businesses.

 Lloyd Augustus Hall invented the first door stop in 1883. This invention made it easier to keep doors open, and it has helped to prevent accidents.

 Elijah McCoy invented the first doorknob that could be operated with one hand in 1890. This invention made it easier for people with disabilities to open doors, and it has helped to improve their independence.

DUST PAN: Sarah Boone invented the first dust pan in 1895. This invention made it easier to sweep up dirt and debris, and it has helped to keep homes and businesses cleaner.

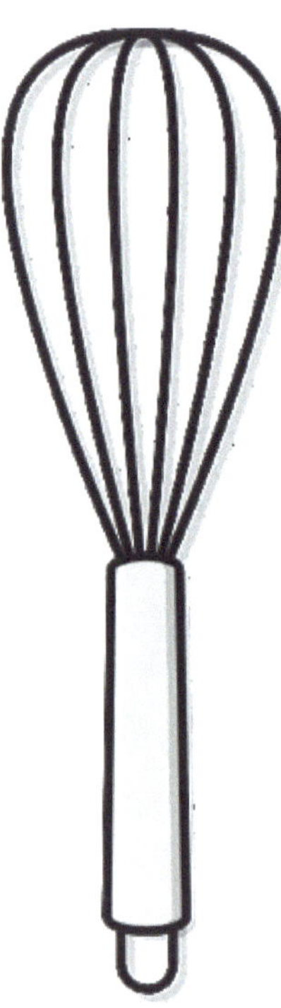

EGG BEATER: Melitta Nicholas invented the first egg beater in 1887. This invention made it easier to beat eggs, and it has helped to improve the taste of cakes, cookies, and other baked goods.

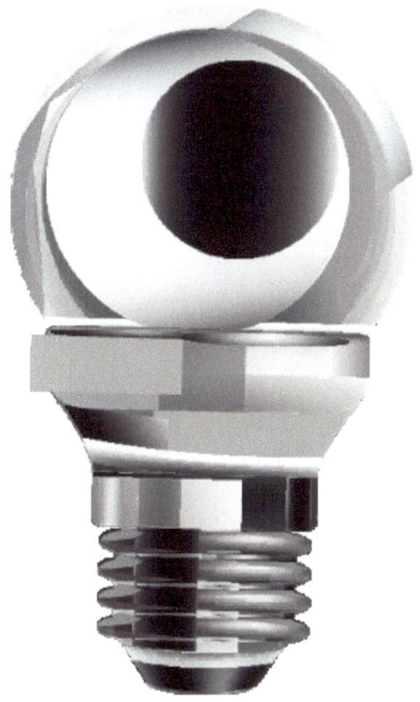

ELECTRIC LAMP BULB: Lewis Latimer invented the carbon filament for the light bulb in 1881. This invention made light bulbs more affordable and efficient, and it helped to usher in the age of electric lighting

ELEVATOR: Alexander Miles invented the first automatic elevator doors in 1887. This invention made elevators safer and more convenient, and it has helped to make tall buildings more accessible.

EYE PROTECTOR: Powell Johnson of Barton, Alabama received a patent for an eye-protector for use by furnace men, firemen, and others exposed to glare of strong light.

FIRE ESCAPE LADDER: William B. Purvis invented the first fire escape ladder in 1887. This invention helped to save countless lives during fires, and it is still used in buildings today.

FIRE EXTINGUISHER: Alfred B. Downing invented the first fire extinguisher in 1866. This invention helped to put out fires more quickly and easily, and it has helped to save countless lives.

FOUNTAIN PEN: Lewis Latimer invented the first fountain pen with a self—fill— Ing mechanism in 1884. This invention made fountain pens more conven— ient to use, and it has helped to make them more popular.

GAS MASK: Garrett Morgan invented the first gas mask in 1912. This invention helped to save countless lives during World War I, and it is still used by firefighters and other first responders today.

GOLF TEE: George F. Grant invented the first golf tee in 1899. This invention made it easier to hit golf balls, and it has helped to improve the game of golf.

 GUITAR: Daniel E. Freeman invented the first guitar with a metal body in 1939. This invention made guitars louder and more durable, and it has helped to make them more popular.

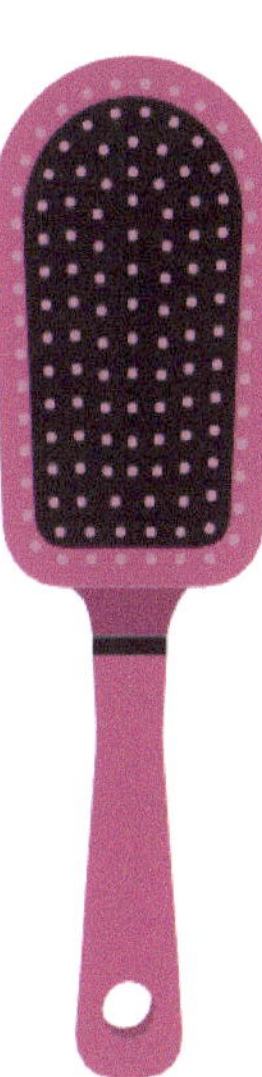

HAIR BRUSH: Sarah Boone invented the first hair brush with a rubber back in 1898. This invention made hair brushes more comfortable to use, and it has helped to improve the health of hair.

HORSESHOE: Jan Ernst Matzeliger invented the first machine that could mass—produce horseshoes in 1883. This invention made horseshoes more affordable and accessible, and it has helped to improve the health and safety of horses.

ICE CREAM SCOOP: Nancy Green invented the first ice cream scoop in 1893. This invention made it easier to scoop ice cream, and it has helped to make ice cream more popular.

IRONING BOARD: Sarah Boone invented the first ironing board with a padded top in 1892. This invention made ironing easier and more comfortable, and it has helped to improve the appearance of clothing.

KEY CHAIN: Elijah McCoy invented the first key chain in 1885. This invention made it easier to keep keys together, and it has helped to prevent people from losing their keys.

LANTERN: Lewis Latimer invented the first lantern with a carbon filament in 1880. This invention made lanterns more effient and durable, and it has helped to improve the safety of people who work in the dark.

LAWN MOWER: John W. Goode invented the first lawn mower with a gasoline engine in 1922. This invention made lawn mowing easier and more effient, and it has helped to make lawns more beautiful.

LAWN SPRINKLER: Joseph R. Landis invented the first lawn sprinkler in 1872. This invention made it easier to water lawns, and it has helped to keep lawns green and healthy.

LEMON SQUEEZER: Lewis Latimer invented the first lemon squeezer with a spring–loaded lever in 1884. This invention made it easier to squeeze lemons, and it has helped to improve the taste of lemonade and other drinks.

LOCK: Elijah McCoy invented the first lock that could be operated with one hand in 1885. This invention made it easier for people with disabilities to use locks, and it has helped to improve their independence.

LUNCH PAIL: Alice H. Parker invented the first lunch pail with a thermos in 1897. This invention made it easier to keep food warm, and it has helped to improve the nutrition of schoolchildren.

MAILBOX: Mary Beatrice Davidson Kenner invented the first mailbox with a hinged door in 1927. This invention made it easier to put mail in mailboxes, and it has helped to improve the effiency of the postal service.

MOP: Thomas W. Stewart invented the first mop with a wringer in 1883. This invention made it easier to wring out mops, and it has helped to improve the cleanliness of floors.

MOTOR: Granville T. Woods invented the first electric motor that could be operated with a single wire in 1886. This invention made electric motors more affordable and accessible, and it has helped to revolutionize the way we power our homes and businesses.

PEANUT BUTTER: George Washington Carver invented the first peanut butter—making machine in 1903. This invention made peanut butter more affordable and accessible, and it has helped to make peanut butter a popular food.

PENCIL SHARPENER: John Wesley Gilbert invented the first pencil sharpener with a rotating blade in 1897. This invention made it easier to sharpen pen– cils, and it has helped to improve the writing experience.

PHONE TRANSMITTER: Granville T. Woods invented the first phone transmitter that could be used with a single wire in 1886. This invention made tele– phones more affordable and accessible, and it has helped to revolutionize the way we communicate.

 Frederick McKinley Jones invented the first portable refrigerator in 1947. This invention made it possible to keep food cold on the go, and it has helped to improve the safety and freshness of food.

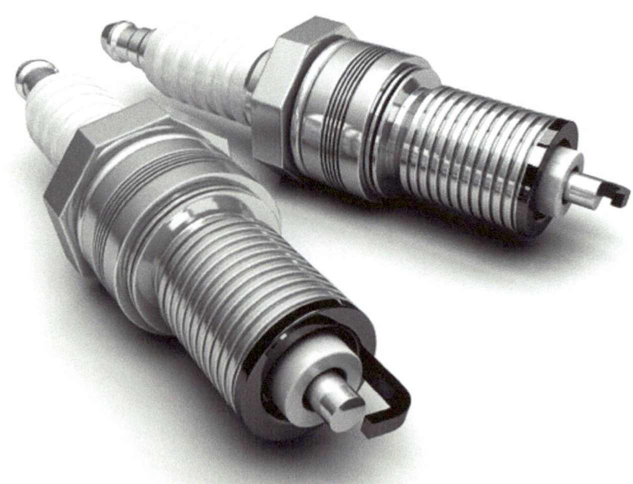

 Elijah McCoy invented the first spark plug with a threaded shell in 1890. This invention made spark plugs more durable and reliable, and it has helped to improve the performance of gasoline engines.

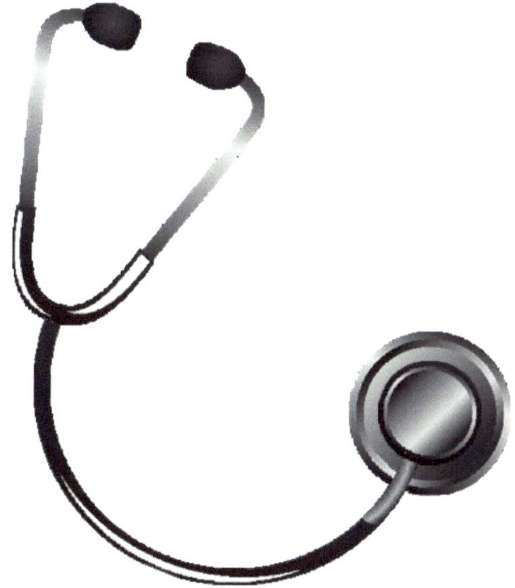

 James Marion Sims invented the first stethoscope with two earpieces in 1851. This invention made it easier to listen to the heart and lungs, and it has helped to improve the diagnosis and treatment of medical conditions.

THERMOSTAT CONTROL: Granville T. Woods invented the first thermostat con—trol that could be operated with a single wire in 1886. This invention made thermostats more affordable and accessible, and it has helped to improve the effiency of heating and cooling systems.

TRICYCLE: In 1888, African American inventor James Pope patented his design for a tricycle, which he called the "Pope Rambler." The tricycle was designed to be more efficient and easier to ride than a bicycle, and it quickly became popular among children and adults alike. Today, tricycles are still used by children for fun and recreation, and they are also used by adults with disabilities as a form of transportation.

TYPEWRITER: In 1878, African American inventor Lewis Latimer patented his design for an improved typewriter, which he called the "Latimer Typewriter." The Latimer Typewriter was easier to use than previous typewriters, and it was also more durable. Today, Latimer is credited with helping to make the typewriter a more practical and affordable tool for businesses and individuals alike.

The contributions of black inventors to American society are vast and varied. From the development of the traffic light to the creation of the peanut butter—making machine, black inventors have made our lives better in countless ways.

If you're interested in learning more about black inventors, there are a wealth of resources available to you. Google, books, and other printed and electronic media all offer information and stories about these trailblazing individuals.

LeoApe™ encourages you to explore these resources and learn more about the important inventions that black inventors have created. You may be sur— prized at just how much you have to learn!

Here are some specific resources that you may find helpful:

- **The National Inventors Hall of Fame:** This Website features biographies of black inventors, as well as information about their inventions.

- **The Blacks Inventors Museum:** This museum in Alexandria, Virginia, houses a collection of artifacts and exhibits related to black inventors.

- **The National Black Technology Project:** This organization provides educational resources and programs about black inventors and technology.

I hope you enjoyed learning about the amazing inventions of black people. These inventors were pioneers who overcame many obstacles to make their mark on the world. Their stories are an inspiration to us all, and I hope they will encourage you to dream big and never give up on your goals.

Thank you for taking the time to read my book. I hope you will share it with your friends and family so that they can learn about these amazing inventors too.

Get your FREE GIFT!!! Join the LeoApe™ Club. https://leoape.com.

Sincerely,

Wallace O Stephens